W9-BKG-866

Alexander Graham **Bell**

Other titles in the Inventors and Creators series include:

Inventors and Creators

Alexander Graham Bell

Deanne Durrett

**KIDHAVEN
PRESS**™

THOMSON
™
GALE

San Diego • Detroit • New York • San Francisco • Cleveland
New Haven, Conn. • Waterville, Maine • London • Munich

Picture Credits:
Cover photo: Library of Congress
© Bettmann/CORBIS, 13, 15, 17, 19, 29
© CORBIS, 30, 40
Library of Congress, 10, 14, 16, 20, 21, 23, 24, 28, 37, 41
© National Portrait Gallery, Smithsonian Institution/Art Resource, NY, 38
Brandy Noon, 9, 35
© North Wind Pictures, 18, 27, 32
© Stock Montage, Inc., 7, 11, 36

© 2003 by KidHaven Press. KidHaven Press is an imprint of The Gale Group, Inc.,
a division of Thomson Learning, Inc.

KidHaven™ and Thomson Learning™ are trademarks used herein under license.

For more information, contact
KidHaven Press
27500 Drake Rd.
Farmington Hills, MI 48331-3535
Or you can visit our Internet site at http://www.gale.com

LIBRARY OF CONGRESS CATALOGING-IN-PUBLICATION DATA

Durrett, Deanne, 1940–
  Alexander Graham Bell / by Deanne Durrett.
    p. cm.—(Inventors and creators)
Includes bibliographical references and index.
Summary: Discusses the early childhood, education, interests, and inventions
of Alexander Graham Bell.
  ISBN 0-7377-0991-X (hardback : alk. paper)
1. Bell, Alexander Graham, 1847–1922—Juvenile literature. 2. Telephone—
History—Juvenile literature. 3. Inventors—United States—Biography—Juvenile
literature. [1. Bell, Alexander Graham, 1847–1922. 2. Inventors.] I. Title. II. Series.
  TK6143 .B4 D87 2003
  621.385'092—dc21

2001006610

Contents

Genius Generalist

Alexander Graham Bell gained his place in history as the inventor of the telephone. Today most people remember him for that reason. Alexander Graham Bell, however, would have been surprised by this. He saw himself as a man with many interests and did not want to limit himself to one specialty. Besides inventing, he was an accomplished pianist. He taught deaf children to speak, and he founded the Bell Telephone Company and the National Geographic Society.

Born in Scotland in 1847, he moved to Canada in 1870 and to the United States in 1871. He became a U.S. citizen in 1882. Throughout his life, he liked to spend time in peaceful, quiet places. In his youth he found such a place in the country outside Edinburgh, Scotland. While living in North America, his quiet place was his summer home in Nova Scotia, Canada. He named this place Beinn Bhreagh, a Gaelic phrase that means "beautiful mountain."

Alexander Graham Bell, inventor of the telephone.

Alexander Graham Bell died on August 2, 1922. He was buried at Beinn Bhreagh, a place where he dreamed about possibilities, many of which became realities in his inventions.

Chapter One

Boy with an Inquiring Mind

Alexander Graham Bell was born in Edinburgh, Scotland, on March 3, 1847, to Eliza Grace (Symonds) and Alexander Melville Bell. His older brother Melville (Melly) was born in 1845, and his younger brother Edward was born in 1848. Aleck (as Alexander was called) and his brothers enjoyed a close relationship. The three of them shared their father's interest in speech and sound. In their youth they did experiments together. Unfortunately, Melly and Edward died at an early age and Aleck would be the only one to have a career in speech and sound.

The Bell Heritage

Aleck's grandfather Alexander Bell was a successful **elocution** teacher in London. He taught proper speech and helped people overcome speech problems such as stammering and lisping. Aleck's father Alexander Melville Bell (Melville) inherited the elder Bell's interest in speech but

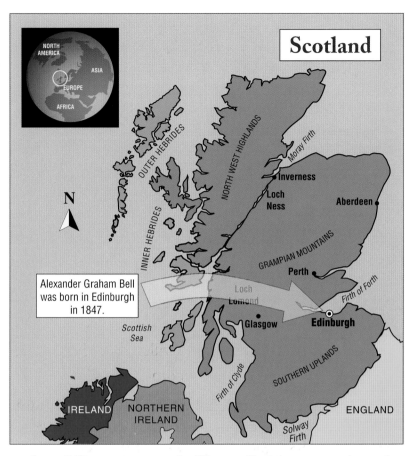

Scotland

Alexander Graham Bell was born in Edinburgh in 1847.

took a different approach. He studied how people make speech sounds and developed a type of phonetic alphabet called Visible Speech. Visible Speech is a series of symbols that represents all the sounds the human mouth can make. He used this system to help **deaf-mutes** learn to communicate. His students were very successful and his research earned him worldwide recognition and respect.

Eliza Bell

Aleck's mother Eliza Grace Symonds Bell was an intelligent and well-read woman. She was also a talented musician and Aleck inherited her musical ability. In his early years he could play by ear and **improvise** at the piano. Eliza gave Aleck his first music lessons. When his talent emerged, she arranged for him to study music under the famous pianist Auguste Benoit Bertini.

Aleck dreamed of becoming a concert pianist. Unfortunately, Bertini died before Aleck had advanced far in his music studies and he never took lessons from another teacher. Still, Aleck enjoyed playing the piano for pleasure throughout his life. His education, however, would lead to a career in his father's field.

Bell (right) and his two brothers pose for a portrait painted by their mother.

Education

Eliza Bell homeschooled Aleck and his brothers through their primary years. Aleck's formal education began in 1857 when he and his younger brother Edward enrolled at Hamilton Place Academy. They later attended Royal High School. Aleck did not enjoy school and was not an outstanding student. Still, the Bell brothers were expected to attend college.

Many students taught high school while studying at the university in Scotland. In 1863, Aleck and his older brother Melly began sharing a teaching position at Weston House Academy in Elgin, Scotland, while they took turns attending the University of Edinburgh. One semester Melly studied at the university while Aleck taught high school. The next semester, Aleck studied at the university while Melly taught high school.

Both boys acquired enough credits to graduate from college. They took courses that would help them in a speech and elocution career. These included intense studies of language including Latin and Greek.

While Aleck's formal education prepared him for a career in speech, his experience at home gave him compassion for the deaf and a desire to help them. It also stirred his interest in the transmission of sound.

Bell attended the University of Edinburgh in Scotland in the 1860s.

Compassion for the Deaf

His mother lost most of her ability to hear by the time Aleck reached his teens. There were no hearing aids at that time so Eliza used a **hearing tube**. When she wanted to hear better, she held the small end of the hearing tube to her ear and directed the large end toward the person speaking. The hearing tube funnels the sound vibrations toward the eardrum. She sometimes pressed the hearing tube against the sounding board of the piano to hear Aleck play.

In his early teens, Aleck concluded that his mother could detect the vibrations of his voice the same way she detected the vibrations of the sounding board. By this time his voice had deepened. He bypassed the hearing tube and spoke close to his mother's forehead in resonant (vibrating) low tones. And she understood his words.

Talking Dog

The understanding of sound that allowed Aleck to help his mother hear made him think about using Mr. Perd (his dog) to experiment with voice. His father encouraged him to experiment. After giving the matter some thought, Aleck taught Mr. Perd to growl on command. Then he experimented by shaping the dog's lips while pressing on the dog's throat. In this way he controlled the flow of air and sound vibrations during the growl. After some practice, Aleck made the dog's growl sound very much like "How are you, Grandmama?"[1]

Melville Bell encouraged Aleck to wonder about the world of sound around him, think about it, and make

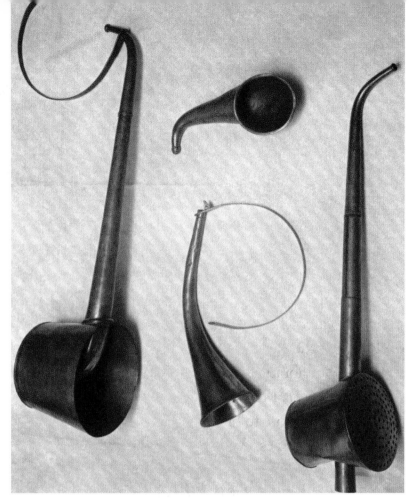

Bell's mother used hearing tubes like these. The thin ends are inserted in the ear; the larger ends increase the volume of sounds.

discoveries. On the practical side, however, he encouraged Aleck and his brothers to participate in his business.

Young Assistants

When Aleck and his brothers were old enough they assisted their father in demonstrating Visible Speech in European lecture halls. The boys could produce any vocal sound by reading Visible Speech symbols. They proved this during their father's lectures.

Bell's father created this Visible Speech chart. The marks represent all of the sounds the human voice can make.

While the boys were out of the room, someone in the audience would suggest a word or make a sound. Professor Bell then wrote the suggestion in Visible Speech on a blackboard. When the boys returned they read the symbols and spoke the word or produced the sound. They were accurate. They could read and produce any sound or words in any language.

While the Bells were demonstrating Visible Speech, Sir Charles Wheatstone was working on a talking machine that could mechanically produce sounds like human speech.

Talking Machine

When Aleck was fifteen, his father took him to visit Wheatstone and see his talking machine. Aleck later said that the sounds made by the machine were not very good. Still, he admitted that "it made a great impression upon my mind."[2] A short time later, Melville Bell challenged his sons to make a better talking machine.

Aleck and Melly tackled the project together. They modeled their creation after human anatomy. Melly created the portion that would act as the lungs and throat with an old bellows-like device from a pump organ for the air source. Aleck constructed the tongue and mouth part from scraps of rubber, wood, wire, and cotton. The boys also fashioned a crude control panel.

When they achieved success, the Bell brothers' talking machine

Sir Charles Wheatstone built a machine that could make the sounds of the human voice.

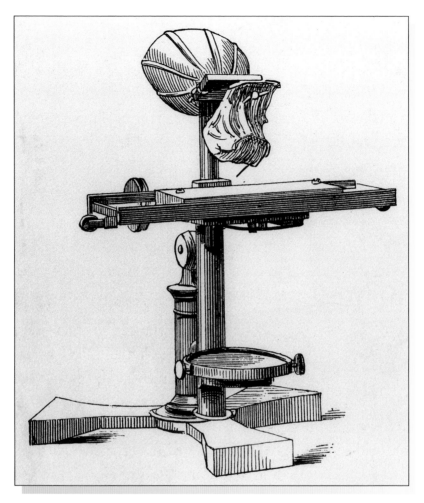

Bell's talking machine was modeled after parts of the human throat and lungs.

produced the sound of a baby crying "Mamma, Mamma." Many years later (in 1909), Alexander Graham Bell wrote that the talking machine "started me along the path that led to the telephone."[3]

Chapter Two

"Mr. Watson— Come Here . . ."

In the mid-1800s, people had to write letters when they wanted to send messages long distance. This took days or weeks depending on how far the letter had to travel. When someone wanted to send a message quickly, he or she would send it by telegraph. The telegraph operator transmitted the message in dots and dashes of electric current called Morse code. The coded message traveled over a wire. The telegraph operator at the receiving end listened to the sound of the dots and dashes, decoded the message, and delivered the telegram.

Two telegraph operators communicate with each other as their messages travel through wires.

Since the telegraph involved sending sound over a wire, Aleck began to wonder if spoken words could be sent over telegraph wires. After college, he earned his living as a teacher at Susanna E. Hull's School for deaf children in Bath, England. In his spare time, however, he dreamed about building a talking telegraph and sometimes made sketches.

Scientific Proof

When Aleck was eighteen, he began to think about human voice sounds in terms of music. He wondered if vowel sounds were a single pitch or a compound pitch. In other words, he wanted to know if a vowel is like one note of music or a chord (several notes sounding together).

Aleck did a scientific experiment to find out. First he tested the pitch of human sounds by comparing them to **tuning forks**. Then he fashioned a device with stretched membranes (something like a drum) to measure the vi-

Workers erect telegraph poles as a carrier on horseback delivers mail.

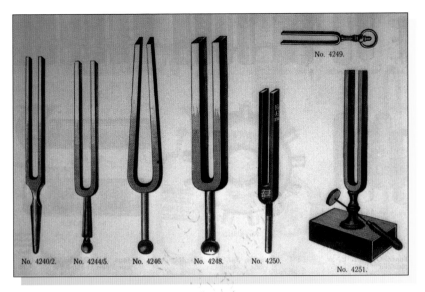

Tuning forks of different sizes vibrate with different pitches when struck.

brations of human speech. He proved that each vowel sound is a compound pitch. He recorded the details of his experiment and presented the paper to his father. Melville Bell encouraged Aleck to send the paper to the leading **phonetics** authority, Alexander John Ellis. Impressed by the paper, Ellis scheduled a meeting with Aleck. Alexander Graham Bell later wrote that after the meeting he became certain that speech would be transmitted by telegraph. While still in his teens, Aleck told his friends that "someday we should talk by telegraph."[4] Before he could begin serious work on the talking telegraph, tragedy struck the Bell family.

Tragedy Strikes

First eighteen-year-old Edward died of tuberculosis in 1867, and then twenty-five-year-old Melly died of the same disease in 1870. When Aleck's health began to fail, his parents urged him to leave the smoggy and crowded cities of England and Scotland and move to Canada with them. Aleck agreed and the Bells moved to North America. They made their new home in Brantford, Ontario, Canada.

After a few weeks of rest in Canada Aleck's health improved greatly, and he accepted a teaching position at the Boston School for the Deaf in Massachusetts. He moved to the United States in 1871 and became a citizen in 1882.

Balancing Act

In Boston, news of Aleck's teaching methods using Visible Speech to help deaf-mutes learn to speak brought invitations to teach classes at other schools. Soon his

Students and teachers at the Boston School for the Deaf. Bell accepted a teaching position there in 1871.

busy schedule left no time for working on the talking telegraph. As a result, he decided to become a private teacher. His plan was to accept a limited number of students and allow himself time for work on the talking telegraph.

Aleck quickly established a reputation as a talented teacher of the deaf, and some of his students came from wealthy families. One student, Georgie, was the deaf son of Thomas Sanders, a successful leather goods merchant. Aleck agreed to tutor Georgie privately at the Sanders's home. During this time, he became good friends with Thomas Sanders. Aleck told Sanders about his work with the talking telegraph and Sanders saw the business potential.

Partnership

Sanders believed that the talking telegraph would compete with the telegraph. A talking message could be sent much faster than spelling the same message out in Morse code. He believed the talking telegraph company would make millions of

Bell decided to be a private teacher so he would have more time to work on his talking telegraph.

dollars and its inventor would go down in history. Sanders made a deal with Bell to finance his experiments and become his partner. Sanders also offered Bell living quarters with room for experiments in his (Sanders) mother's home. Once Bell accepted, Sanders also moved Georgie to his mother's home as well.

This arrangement suited Bell. He taught other students during the day, tutored Georgie in the evenings, and had the nights free to work on the talking telegraph. Alexander Graham Bell enjoyed his work. Throughout his life, he routinely worked long into the night.

Third Partner

Materials for Bell's experiments proved to be expensive. Before long Sanders and Bell welcomed Gardiner Green Hubbard as the third partner. He was the father of a young woman Bell tutored, Mabel Hubbard. As a **patent** attorney and businessman, Gardiner Hubbard brought additional funds and knowledge into the partnership.

Hubbard believed that the multiple telegraph, or a telegraph that could send several messages over one wire, would be the next great invention. Consequently, he insisted that Bell work on this project. In need of Hubbard's money and knowledge of patents, Bell agreed. Hubbard and Bell formed a lifelong relationship. And, Aleck soon fell in love with Hubbard's deaf daughter, Mabel.

Aleck decided to keep his feelings for Mabel secret until he could afford to support her. His income from teaching barely paid his own expenses. His only hope for more income lay in a successful invention.

Bell listens closely to hear if someone's voice has been transmitted through the wire.

An Assistant

Bell was good at thinking and designing experimental devices. He was not good at building the devices he sketched on paper. With this in mind, he found a young man with mechanical talent to help him. Bell's new assistant Thomas Watson also knew about electricity.

Combining their skills and knowledge, Bell and Watson tried to send multiple messages in different tones over one wire. This invention, which Bell called the harmonic telegraph, failed.

The Telephone

While working on the harmonic telegraph, however, Bell recalled his experiment that used a membrane to recreate the vibrations of the human voice. He switched

Two actors portray Bell (left) and Thomas Watson as they discuss the invention of the telephone.

projects and added a membrane device to his talking telegraph. After some adjusting, tinkering, and further experimenting, on March 10, 1876, he achieved the success that would make him famous. Bell was in one room with the **transmitter**. Watson was in another room with the **receiver** earpiece pressed to his ear. The doors of both rooms were closed. Bell spoke into the mouthpiece. And Watson heard the words that would go down in history as the first telephone message, "Mr. Watson— Come here—I want to see you."[5]

Chapter Three

Bell Telephone Company and Beyond

O nce Alexander Graham Bell succeeded in transmitting human speech with his talking telegraph (telephone), he was ready to concentrate on his deaf students again. When the opportunity came to demonstrate the new invention at the 1876 Centennial Exhibition in Philadelphia, Bell did not want to go. His students were taking tests and he did not want to leave them. It did not matter to him that this was the first World's Fair in the United States. It would attract visitors from distant places, so demonstrating a new invention at the Centennial Exhibition offered far more than the possibility of winning a prize at the fair. It was an opportunity to introduce the telephone to the world.

At Hubbard's and Sanders's insistence, Bell agreed to attend the exhibition for one day only—Sunday, June 25, 1876. Bell later explained in a speech that he "was not very much alive to commercial matters . . . and could not be bothered by having to go to Philadelphia."[6]

1876 Centennial Exhibition

That Sunday, the telephone was scheduled to be the last demonstration. It was a hot day, and toward evening the judges decided to postpone the demonstration of the telephone until the next morning. One judge, Dom Pedro II, emperor of Brazil, expressed interest in the new invention. Bell quickly demonstrated it for him and Sir William Thompson, a noted English scientist, who was standing nearby. Unfortunately, when the exhibit hall closed for the day the telephone had to be taken apart and moved. Sticking to his plan, Bell left for Boston before it could be reassembled. As a result, only Emperor Pedro II and Sir William Thompson witnessed Bell's demonstration.

A crowd excitedly passes through the entrance of the 1876 Centennial Exhibition in Philadelphia, Pennsylvania.

Bell demonstrates his telephone to Brazilian emperor Dom Pedro II at the Centennial Exhibition.

Still, the potential for this invention was so great, once these two people had seen it, the news spread. Bell said later, in a speech, "from that time dates the popular interest in the telephone."[7]

Bell Telephone Company

Bell and his partners formed the Bell Telephone Company in 1877. The first telephone exchange began operating in New Haven, Connecticut, in 1878.

By 1885 the telephone was well established in local exchanges across the nation. Once the telephone became a dependable device used in many homes, the company was on the way to becoming a gigantic financial success.

The Bell Telephone Company expanded to become the American Bell Telephone Company. With this expansion, a network was needed to connect these exchanges and offer long-distance service between cities. On March 3, 1885, the American Bell Telephone Company created a **subsidiary** company to do the job. They named this subsidiary the American Telephone and Telegraph Company (AT&T). In the next thirty years long-distance service would stretch from coast to coast.

Mr. and Mrs. Alexander Graham Bell

With this financial security in their future, Aleck and Mabel were married on July 11, 1877. She was nineteen and he was thirty. On their wedding day, Aleck gave Mabel 1,497 shares of Bell Telephone stock, all but 10

Telephone operators are busy at work at the Bell Telephone Company.

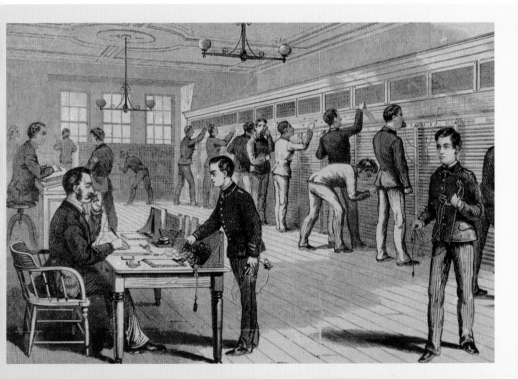

Aleck and Mabel married once Bell's company had proven its worth.

shares of his holdings in the new company. Knowing he lacked business sense, he placed the family finances in her capable hands.

Mabel and Aleck would have four children. Elsie May arrived in 1878. Marian, whom they called Daisy, followed in 1880. Two sons died shortly after birth; Edward in 1881 and Robert in 1883.

The first year of their marriage, Aleck and Mabel lived in England while Aleck lectured and demonstrated the telephone in Europe. Soon European nations recognized the importance of Bell's invention. The first British telephone exchange began operation in London in 1879.

Volta Prize

In the fall of 1880, the French government honored Bell with the Volta Prize. The Volta Prize gave Bell recognition for inventing the telephone. It included fifty thousand francs (French currency equaling about ten thousand American dollars). With this money and recognition, Bell put his success with the telephone in the past and moved on to other interests. These included working on inventions designed to ease human suffering and save lives.

Humanitarian Efforts

Many considered Alexander Graham Bell to be a humanitarian above all else. This means that he cared about people, especially those who were hurting. He thought that "relieving suffering and saving life"[8] was a good reason to spend long hours working on an invention.

Bell put these words into action in 1881 when he tried to save the life of U.S. president James Garfield. During an assassination attempt, a bullet lodged deep in President Garfield's back. Doctors could not locate the bullet. They knew of Bell's reputation as an inventor and asked him to create a device that could find the bullet. Bell designed a magnetic device that detected bullets in tests and also in other patients.

It was not successful, however, in finding the president's bullet. As it turned out, a steel mesh pad under the president's bedding had interfered with the magnetic device. President Garfield died from infection and loss of blood on September 19, 1881. Bell's bullet probe went on to save countless lives from that time until after World War I when X rays came into use.

That same year, Bell's newborn son Edward died from breathing difficulties. Premature babies have immature lungs. Not ready to breathe on their own, they often suffer breathing difficulties. While mourning the loss of his son, Bell worked on a vest designed to save other babies with this problem. He designed this device

Bell (right) uses one of his inventions to try to find a bullet lodged in President Garfield's back.

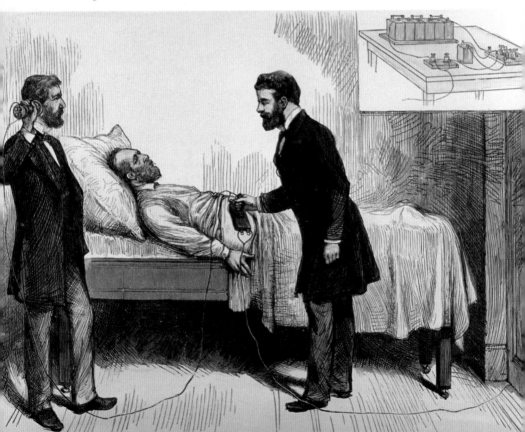

to fit around the chest and force air in and out of the lungs. The vest, however, was not successful. Still, Bell was on the right track. Philip Drinker would use the same technology in 1928 to invent the **iron lung**. This device would save the lives of many polio victims in the mid-1900s. In experiments such as this and in many of his sketched ideas, Bell was ahead of his time. As a result, he invested time and money in many ideas that produced no income for him.

Financial Success

The success of the telephone company, however, supported Bell's experiments and humanitarian efforts. It also allowed him to find his dreaming place. With some of their telephone wealth, the Bells began buying land on Cape Breton Island in Nova Scotia in 1886. Eventually, they would build an elegant summer home there called Beinn Bhreagh, a peaceful place where Bell would pursue other interests including experiments in flight.

Chapter Four

The Idea Man

At Beinn Bhreagh, Bell built and flew kites and imagined the possibilities. As the result, more than nine years before the Wright brothers made the first flight at Kitty Hawk, North Carolina, Bell told a reporter that he believed that "the problem of aerial navigation [flight] will be solved within ten years."[9]

Bell made kites of all sizes, shapes, and designs. These kites were not toys; they were experiments in the dynamics of flight. By flying differently shaped kites, Bell studied lift, which is the force that raises a kite from the ground. He also studied wind flow, the way the air currents moved around, above, and below each kite. This information is important in designing aircraft that will rise from the ground, stay aloft, and land safely.

The Tetrahedron

While trying to build a kite that would lift a man into the air, Bell experimented with many shapes. He wanted to find a way to design a kite with more lift that weighed less. During this search, Bell discovered the strength of the **tetrahedron** in 1901. The tetrahedron is made of rods joined to form four triangles—three that form a pyramid with the fourth at the bottom. Bell made huge kites using tetrahedron cells, some shaped like airplanes.

The tetrahedron is a strong and stable construction design that can be fitted together to form almost any shape.

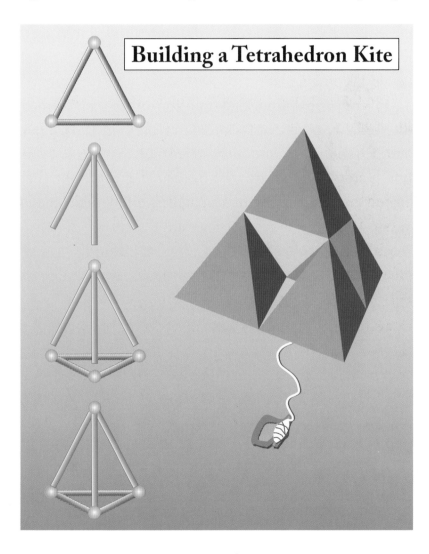

Building a Tetrahedron Kite

It is especially important where strength with less weight is desirable. It is used in building bridges and towers.

While Bell experimented with kites and shapes, Wilbur and Orville Wright would be the first to design an airplane that would lift a man into the air.

The *Silver Dart*

The Wright brothers made the first flight at Kitty Hawk in 1903. From takeoff to landing, that engine-powered plane was in the air 12 seconds and traveled 120 feet. Many improvements were needed before air travel would become a reality.

With this in mind, Bell and four other men formed the Aerial Experiment Association (AEA) in 1907. They built a series of experimental airplanes that made aviation history. The fourth, the *Silver Dart,* made the first engine-powered flight in Canada in 1909. That plane

The Wright brothers test their engine-powered plane at Kitty Hawk, North Carolina, in 1903.

The crew of the *Silver Dart* tries to launch their plane from a frozen lake in 1909.

took off, reached an altitude of thirty feet, and traveled almost a mile before touching down.

From kites to the flight of the *Silver Dart*, Bell had a long-term interest in flight. His inventions contributed to better landing gears (tricycle undercarriage) and flight control equipment (the **aileron**).

As the years passed, Bell continued working on his experiments. His mind remained sharp and he continued working long hours. When he was about sixty-eight, Bell explained to a reporter that mental ability would not decrease as long as a person "continues to observe, to remember what he [or she] observes, and to seek answers for his [or her] unceasing hows and whys about things."[10]

Hydrofoil

The last ten years of his life, Bell worked on improving the hydrofoil. A hydrofoil is a boat that hovers over the surface of the water. A hydrofoil has wings (foils) that fly in the water (hydro). The hydrofoil wings lift the hull of the boat out of the water (like wings lift an airplane off

Bell continued to work on experiments during the last years of his life.

the runway). With its hull raised and only its wings in the water, the hydrofoil is much faster than other boats. Bell hoped that the hydrofoil might be fast enough to catch and destroy German submarines that were sinking U.S. ships during World War I. Bell was unsuccessful in building a "submarine chaser" to meet military needs. He did, however, build a hydrofoil that set a world speed record of seventy-one miles per hour on September 9, 1919. At the age of seventy-two, Alexander Graham Bell owned a patent on the fastest boat in the world. Improving the hydrofoil would be Bell's last project.

Bell's Death

Alexander Graham Bell was diagnosed with **diabetes** in 1920. He also suffered from **anemia**. Still, he continued his normal routine and showed few symptoms of his illness until shortly before his death. On July 30, 1922, he helped test another experimental hydrofoil. The next day he weakened and went to bed. Alexander Graham Bell died on August 2, 1922, with Mabel at his side, her hand in his.

Alexander Graham Bell is buried at his summer home, Beinn Bhreagh, in Nova Scotia

Mechanical Genius

Bell was interested in the whole world of mechanics and technology. He was a mechanical genius who could see a task that needed to be done and design a device to do it. Few of his inventions were overnight successes. Most took years to perfect.

During this time, he worked on several projects—applying ideas to each as they came to him.

Bell was ahead of his time. He understood principles of technology that would not become a reality for decades. For example, his photophone transmitted sound on a light beam, a technology that eventually would be developed into fiber optics.

Bell also tinkered with the technology involved in solar energy and computers. He encouraged new approaches to education and warned of fuel shortages, the greenhouse effect, and global warming.

Bell spent summers at his home in Nova Scotia and died there in 1922.

Bell makes the first long-distance call from New York to Chicago in 1892.

During his life, Bell worked on hundreds of projects and received numerous patents on the resulting inventions. His work contributed to better airplanes, faster boats, stronger bridges, and taller towers. He was an idea man who thought about possibilities. Projects that seemed to have failed simply may be projects he did not finish. Only one, however, brought him fortune and fame—the telephone.

Notes

Chapter 1: Boy with an Inquiring Mind

1. Quoted in Edwin S. Grosvenor and Morgan Wesson, *Alexander Graham Bell: The Life and Times of the Man Who Invented the Telephone.* New York: Harry N. Abrams, 1997, p. 29.

2. Quoted in Grosvenor and Wesson, *Alexander Graham Bell,* p. 17.

3. Quoted in Grosvenor and Wesson, *Alexander Graham Bell,* p. 23.

Chapter 2: "Mr. Watson—Come Here . . ."

4. Quoted in Grosvenor and Wesson, *Alexander Graham Bell,* p. 30.

5. Alexander Graham Bell, Alexander Graham Bell Family Papers, American Memories Collection, March 10, 1876, Library of Congress. http://memory.loc.gov.

Chapter 3: Bell Telephone Company and Beyond

6. Bell, Alexander Graham Bell Family Papers, November 2, 1911, p. 8.

7. Bell, Alexander Graham Bell Family Papers, November 2, 1911, p. 11.

8. Quoted in Grosvenor and Wesson, *Alexander Graham Bell,* p. 108.

Chapter 4: The Idea Man

9. Quoted in Grosvenor and Wesson, *Alexander Graham Bell*, p. 141.

10. Bell, Alexander Graham Bell Family Papers, March 10, 1876, p. 11.

Glossary

aileron: A hinged section on the trailing edge of an airplane wing that controls the plane's rolling movements.

anemia: A condition in which a person has a low red blood cell count.

deaf-mute: A person who cannot hear or speak.

diabetes: A disorder in which the pancreas does not produce enough insulin for the body to process sugars.

elocution: The art of public speaking.

hearing tube: A horn-shaped instrument that directs sounds to the user's ear.

improvise: To make something up on the spot such as music or lines in a play.

iron lung: A metal breathing machine that encloses the whole body except for the head and provides artificial respiration for those with severe breathing difficulties.

patent: An official document that prevents others from copying an inventor's invention and marketing it as their own.

phonetics: The study of language and the written symbols that represent the sounds of speech.

receiver: The part of the telephone one presses to the ear.

subsidiary: A company owned and controlled by another company.

tetrahedron: A four-sided shape with three triangles forming a pyramid with a fourth for the bottom.

transmitter: The part of the telephone one holds near the mouth.

tuning fork: A two-pronged tool that vibrates at a certain pitch when struck.

For Further Exploration

Leonard Everett Fisher, *Alexander Graham Bell*. New York: Atheneum, 1999. A storylike account of Alexander Graham Bell's life covering his personal life, work with the deaf, and inventions.

Sarah Gearhart, *The Telephone (Turning Point Inventions)*. New York: Atheneum, 1999. This book explores the world before the telephone, its invention, and its influence. It also details how the telephone works.

John Langone and Pete Samek, *National Geographic's How Things Work: Everyday Technology Explained*. Washington, DC: National Geographic Society, 1999. This books explains how things work and gives some idea of how the inventors connected wires, wheels, gadgets, and gizmos to create things of wonder.

Peter Mellett, *Flight (Fantastic Facts)*. Southwater Pub, 2000. This book is a collection of interesting experiments that encourage scientific thinking and offer insight into realistic scientific work.

Index